The

60

Minute
Investment
Guide

What You Need to Know to Manage Your
Money in Easily Understood Language,
and All in Only 1 Hour

MICHAEL L. WALDEN, PH.D.

Atlantic Publishing Group, Inc.

THE 60-MINUTE INVESTMENT GUIDE: WHAT YOU NEED TO KNOW TO MANAGE YOUR MONEY IN EASILY UNDERSTOOD LANGUAGE, AND ALL IN ONLY 1 HOUR

1210 SW 23rd PL • Ocala, FL 34471 • Phone 352-622-1825
Website: www.atlantic-pub.com • Email: sales@atlantic-pub.com
SAN Number: 268-1250

Library of Congress Control Number: 2023918679

Printed in the United States

PROJECT MANAGER: Crystal Edwards
INTERIOR LAYOUT AND JACKET DESIGN: Nicole Sturk

Table of Contents

Acknowledgements

I thank the wonderful professionals at Atlantic Publishing Group who shepherded the book from the initial manuscript to the final copy. I also thank Bogdan Nikiforov for help with the computer programs associated with the book. And, as always, thanks to my wife Mary for her support and insightful comments.

Introduction

We all live for both today and tomorrow. Investing is about tomorrow. Investing means we take money we have today, and, rather than spend it, put the money to work so that it may grow to become a larger amount in the future. We then use that larger amount of money for some goal, like buying a home or vehicle, paying for a child's education, or funding our retirement.

There are three key questions to answer when looking to invest.

The first is how much you'd need to save per established period to reach a certain monetary goal. For example, you must determine how much you'd need to save per month in order to accumulate the $20,000 needed fifteen years from now for one year of your child's college tuition.

The second question to answer is where to invest your money. There are many investment alternatives; stocks, bonds, CD's (certificates of deposit), gold, and real estate are some common examples. Which investment, or combination of investments, is best for your situation, and how can you determine that?

The third question is how to withdraw the money you've invested once you've reached your goal. For many investments, it might be as easy as withdrawing the $20,000 to pay the college tuition or make a down payment on your new home. But for retirement investments, things get a bit trickier because it involves using the funds over many years.

I've written this book so you can get through it in just 60 minutes. It's written using language that anyone can understand so you don't need a degree in economics, finance, or in anything at all to learn applicable financial knowledge. This book offers simple guidelines you can reference when investment decisions arise, and I give you access to online computer programs to generate answers for your specific situations. My goal with this book is to *empower* you to manage and control your investments, even if you already use an advisor. You'll know the right questions to ask, be able to evaluate the answers, and take control of your financial goals.

So, set the timer. In no more than an hour of reading, you'll learn how to be in charge of your investments.

CHAPTER 1

How Much to Invest
for a Specific Purpose

There are seven things to know in order to determine how much to save and invest each month for a future financial goal. You need to know:

1) The amount of money you're hoping to achieve in the future,
2) How many years the amount will be necessary
3) Use 0 if only one year is needed; 1 if multiple years are needed,
4) the percentage of annual interest earned on your investment,
5) the number of years you have in which to invest,
6) the amount of money you've already saved toward your goal, and
7) your tax rate, expressed as a percentage.

Number 7 isn't as self-explanatory as some of the others. Your tax rate is simply the percentage of investments and/or earnings taxed away by federal and state income taxes. The federal rate depends on your total income as well as whether you are single or married. State income taxes also often have separate rates for income and marital status. Current federal tax rates can be found at: *https://www.irs.gov/newsroom/ irs-provides-tax-inflation-adjustments-for-tax-year-2023.*

It's important to note that the rates change each year to adjust for inflation, which can prevent you from being pushed into a higher tax rate bracket just because your earnings kept pace with inflation.

Unless you live in one of the seven states (Alaska, Florida, Nevada, Tennessee, Texas, South Dakota, and Wyoming) that have no state income tax, you'll need to check with your state Department of Revenue or the Tax Foundation to find your state income tax rate.[1] Most are much lower than the federal rates.

---

1. The Tax Foundation is a non-partisan organization founded in 1937 that provides information about both national and state taxes. Their annual report, *Facts and Figures: How Does Your State Compare*, provides current income tax rates for each state. Go to *taxfoundation.com* for information.

Price inflation is another unfortunate fact of economic life to consider. We have no perfect way of predicting inflation, but don't worry. I've developed a computer program that allows you to check on the price of your future purchase each year and recalculate how much you need to save in the remaining years.

The computer program, called *"How Much To Save"*, is available at *www.60minuteinvestmentguide.wordpress.com.*

Here are some examples using *"How Much To Save."*

EXAMPLE 1

Saving for a home down payment

You want to purchase a home in five years. If you bought the home today it would cost $300,000 and the typical 5% down-payment would be $15,000. You need the $15,000 for only one year.

TABLE 1

Saving for a Home Down Payment: Initial Calculation.

Future Amount Needed, Today's $	15,000
Number of Years Future Amount Needed	1
Enter 0 if Only One Year Needed; Enter 1 if More Years Are Needed	0
Annual Interest Rate Earned on Investments, %	5
Number of Years to Invest	5
Amount Already Saved	0
Tax Rate, %	22
Monthly Amount to Save	**$226.82**

The current interest rate you can earn on invested money is 5%, your tax rate is 22%, and you've not yet saved any funds toward your goal.

Table 1 shows these inputs in the "*How Much To Save*" program and indicates that you would need to save and invest $226.82 each month to accumulate $15,000 at the end of five years.

But housing prices usually rise each year. What if, after a year of saving, you check on the same house and find it now costs

$325,000? The required down-payment would be $16,250. You would now need to save more in the remaining four years, but how much more? No problem—just go to the *"How Much To Save"* program and adjust the future amount needed to $16,250, the number of years to invest to 4, and include the $2771[2] you should have already accumulated in the first year of saving (all highlighted in Table 2).

TABLE 2

Saving for a Home Down Payment:
Revised Calculation for Year 2.

Future Amount Needed, Today's $	16,250
Number of Years Future Amount Needed	1
Enter 0 if Only One Year Needed; Enter 1 if More Years Are Needed	0
Annual Interest Rate Earned on Investments, %	5
Number of Years to Invest	4
Amount Already Saved	2771
Tax Rate When Investing, %	22
Monthly Amount to Save	**$259.93**

---

2. Based on saving $226.82 each month for twelve months, earning a 5% annual interest rate, and with a 22% tax bracket. The easiest way to obtain this number is to just check the total in your investment account after a year.

Table 2 shows that you now need to save $259.93 per month for the remaining four years.

Each year you should repeat the calculations to keep up with how housing prices are changing. Another reason to annually update your savings calculations is in the event the returns on your investments aren't what you expected. If they were higher, you can reduce your monthly savings; but if the returns were lower, you will need to increase your monthly saving to meet your goal.

EXAMPLE 2

Saving for College Tuition

Saving for a child's college education is something many parents worry about. As an example, assume your child will start college in 15 years. You want to save enough to have the cost of four years of tuition and fees accumulated by the time college begins. If current annual tuition and fees are $20,000, how much will you need to save and invest monthly if the interest rate earned from investing is 6% and your tax rate is 32%?

TABLE 3

Saving for a College Education: Initial Calculation.

Future Amount Needed, Today's $	20,000
Number of Years Future Amount Needed	4
Enter 0 if Only One Year Needed; Enter 1 if More Years Are Needed	1
Annual Interest Rate Earned on Investments, %	6
Number of Years to Invest	15
Amount Already Saved	0
Tax Rate When Investing, %	32
Monthly Amount to Save	**$304.46**

TABLE 4

Saving for a College Education: Revised Calculation.

Future Amount Needed, Today's $	25,000
Number of Years Future Amount Needed	4
Enter 0 if Only One Year Needed; Enter 1 if More Years Are Needed	1
Annual Interest Rate Earned on Investments, %	6
Number of Years to Invest	10
Amount Already Saved	20226
Tax Rate When Investing, %	32
Monthly Amount to Save	**$500.74**

Table 3 shows the inputs to the *"How Much To Save"* for the initial calculation. Notice the "number of years future amount is needed" is now 4—"1" is used for the third entry because the $20,000 annual amount is needed for four years, and the number of years to invest is "15." The answer is that you must save $304.46 each month.

But since your child's college education is fifteen years away, it's expected that college costs will change. Suppose that after five years of saving for college, you find that annual college tuition and fees were raised to $25,000. You'll need to adjust your monthly amount to save in two ways. You'll need to lower the years for saving to 10. Also, you'll need to include the $20,226 you will have already saved in the past five years.

Table 4 shows that with these changes, the required monthly savings amount is now $500.74 for the remaining ten years. But if college costs change again before your child enters, more updates should be done. Fortunately, they take only seconds.

EXAMPLE 3

Saving for Retirement

If you want to have an enjoyable retirement, you'll likely need to invest for that eventuality while you're working. Although most of us will receive Social Security checks when we retire, those checks probably won't be enough. Indeed, when Social Security was created, it was never meant to be a person's only source of financial support in retirement. According to the Social Security Administration, on average, benefits only cover 40% of what you earned while working![3]

---

3. www.ssa.gov/planners/retire

Therefore, you will need to put some money aside while you're working for your retirement if you intend to maintain your regular lifestyle. The first step in determining how much you must save for your retirement is to estimate how much money you will need each year for living expenses. If you're young and have children at home, you'll want to eliminate child expenses because the children will be on their own by that time…you hope!

TABLE 5

Saving for Retirement: Initial Calculation.

Future Amount Needed, Today's $	38,400
Number of Years Future Amount Needed	30
Enter 0 if Only One Year Needed; Enter 1 if More Years Are Needed	1
Annual Interest Rate Earned on Investments, %	5
Number of Years to Invest	35
Amount Already Saved	0
Tax Rate When Investing, %	32
Monthly Amount to Save, Including Taxes	**$1350.51**
After-Tax Amount at Retiring	**$739,503**

TABLE 6

Saving for Retirement: 2nd Year Revision.

Future Amount Needed, Today's $	40,320
Number of Years Future Amount Needed	30
Enter 0 if Only One Year Needed; Enter 1 if More Years Are Needed	1
Annual Interest Rate Earned on Investments, %	5
Number of Years to Invest	34
Amount Already Saved	11,207
Tax Rate When Investing, %	32
Monthly Amount to Save, Including Taxes	**$1468.06**
After-Tax Amount at Retiring	**$776,478**

After subtracting those expenses, a good rule of thumb is that you'll need approximately 80% of the expenses you had while you were working.

As an example, let's say your annual expenses today are $80,000, not including children. Eighty percent of $80,000 is $64,000. If Social Security is expected to fund 40% of this amount, you'll need to generate enough savings to fund

$38,400 (0.60 x $64,000) for each year in retirement. I recommend planning for at least 30 years in retirement.

I have a computer program named *"Retirement Savings-Regular,"*—also available at *www.60minuteinvestmentguide.wordpress.com*—that calculates how much you will need to save each month to meet your retirement goal. It works similarly to the *"How Much to Save Program"* except its focus is on the long term needs of retirement rather than an individual goal.

Table 5 gives the setup for the previous example of a household needing to generate $38,400 each year for 30 years and having 35 years in which to save. The *"Retirement Savings-Regular"* program calculates that $1,350.51 is your monthly retirement saving requirement. I've included the taxes paid on this amount because the alternative retirement saving plans I discuss next have tax-saving advantages. With a 32% tax rate, the amount invested is actually $918.35.

Notice there a second output from the program called "After-Tax Amount at Retiring." That is the accumulation of your retirement saving at the year you retire. It's important to know this amount when you begin drawing from your retirement savings. This topic is discussed more fully in Chapter 3.

Since inflation occurs almost every year, I strongly recommend you annually revise your retirement savings calculation to account for the past year's inflation. Table 6 shows the second year revision with a 5% overall inflation rate in the first year of saving. Your annual amount needed is now 5% higher, at $40,320. You also have one less year to save. And don't forget to include what you've saved in the first year, which is $11,207 in the example, including interest earnings.[4]

TABLE 7

Taxation of Alternative Retirement Saving Options

	Contribution	Earnings	Withdrawal
Typical Investment	Taxed	Taxed	No Taxes
Regular IRA, 401K, 403B, and Keogh plans	No Taxes	No Taxes	All Taxed
Roth IRA	Taxed	No Taxes	No Taxes

---

4. Based on investing $918.15—the monthly amount after subtracting the 32% tax rate on $1350.51.

The revised monthly amount is now $1,468.06, including taxes paid on the monthly amount.

The retirement calculations given above include the taxes you'll pay on both your investments and withdrawals, assuming they are taxed like any ordinary investment. Fortunately, the federal government has approved several special retirement investments that receive favorable tax treatment and make saving easier.

Table 7 shows the favorable treatments for these special retirement investments compared to a regular investment. With a regular investment (first row, and the one used in Tables 5 and 6), both your contributions and earnings are taxed, but no taxes are paid when you withdraw and use the money.[5]

The second row shows four types of special retirement investments with tax savings. Regular IRAs (individual retirement accounts) are for anyone, 401K plans are offered through private employers, 403B plans are offered through public employers, and Keogh plans are for self-employed persons.

---

5. Remember that funds not yet withdrawn from your retirement saving account that continue to earn money will also have those earnings taxed. The computer programs used for your calculations account for this fact.

Each of these has specific rules about how much you can periodically invest, when you can withdraw the money, how the money may be used, and whether your employer may contribute to your savings. The Appendix gives summaries of the details. What the plans have in common is their tax treatment: contributions and earnings are not taxed, but both are taxed when funds are withdrawn.

The third row shows another type of plan that can be used for retirement called the Roth IRA. The unique feature of the Roth IRA is that everything is taxed upfront when you invest the funds; neither earnings nor withdrawals are taxed.

At *www.60minuteinvestmentguide.wordpress.com,* I've provided you with a separate computer program called *"Retirement Saving – Reg IRA, 401K, 403B, Keogh"* to calculate how much you would need to save for retirement using one of the second group of plans—Regular IRA, 401K, 403B, and Keogh. I've also given you a program to calculate what you would need to save using a Roth IRA called *"Retirement Savings -Roth IRA."*

Using the tax-favored retirement programs clearly saves you money. Let's revisit Table 5, which shows a required monthly retirement savings of $1,350.51 for a regular savings plan.

Applying the same input information to both the *Retirement Savings-Regular IRA, 401K, 403B, Keogh*" program and to the "*Retirement Saving-Roth IRA*" shows a needed monthly saving amount of $957.23 for each, including taxes. It is to your benefit to use one of the tax-favored programs for your retirement savings. Both retirement savings programs are available at *www.60minuteinvestmentguide.wordpress.com.*

Understand that there are limits to all tax-favored savings programs, as you'll see in the Appendix. One of the biggest limitations is federal penalties on withdrawing funds from the investments prior to a certain age—usually 59 and a half years old. The penalty can be as high as 10% on the amount withdrawn, with the penalty paid to the IRS. There are also limits on how much you can invest each year. Still, I recommend you consider the tax-favored programs first. If you're worried about not having access to funds prior to retiring in the tax-favored plans, or if the tax-favored plans won't provide you with enough retirement money, you can always put some money in them and the rest in a regular savings plan.

You'll also need to annually update your retirement savings for inflation with the tax-favored plans, just like you would do with a regular savings plan.

Even though all the tax-favored plans give the same savings answer, you'll hear some financial advisors recommend the Roth IRA due to the fact all taxes are paid upfront when funds are invested. Why would they recommend the Roth? Because they're assuming tax rates will rise in the future. If so, it is better to pay the lower tax rates today than the higher rates later. However, there's no way to accurately predict future tax rates. All sorts of things could happen. Sure, tax rates on income could rise, but they could also drop, as they have in the past at both the federal and state levels. But if you're convinced tax rates will rise, then by all means use a Roth IRA for retirement saving.

CHAPTER 2

Where to Invest

There are two major approaches to investing. One is "beat the market." Here the goal is to continually move your savings to investments earning the best returns. Some people try to do this themselves but many hire financial professionals like stockbrokers, bankers, or personal finance experts.

The second approach is "accept the market." Investors following this approach believe consistently "beating the market" is impossible. Indeed, sometimes attempting to "beat the market" will produce lower, not higher, investment earnings. In a famous study, Nobel Prize winning economist William Sharpe found an investor had to accurately predict the ups and downs in the economy 74% of the time for the "beat the market" approach to produce higher gains than the "accept the market" strategy.[6]

---

6. Sharpe, William, "Likely Gains from Market Timing," *Financial Analysts Journal*, Vol. 31, No. 2, March/April, 1975, pp. 60-69.

In practice, "accept the market" means spreading your savings among the major investment categories and not making changes as economic conditions change. The only changes are altering the percentage of your savings allocated to each investment category as you move through the stages of life.

A great way to do this is avoid buying individual investments, like specific stocks, bonds, or CDs (bank certificates of deposit); instead buy a bundle of individual investments. For example, if you buy a variety of stocks rather than a couple, your investments find safety in numbers. Furthermore, there will be several of these bundles, with each bundle representing a specific type of investment—stocks, bonds, and real estate, etc. This gives another level of safety in numbers. The technical term of this procedure is "diversification." You will have two levels of diversification—across one kind of investment (for example, numerous individual stocks), as well as across many types of investments (like stocks, bonds, and real estate).

I recommend thinking about four broad categories of investments—stocks, inflation hedges, long-term bonds, and cash. A stock represents partial ownership of a company. If the company prospers, so do the owners with a rise in stock value. But if a company falters, its stock value will fall. Most stocks do well when the economy is growing, but many lose when the economy goes into a recession.

Inflation hedges include commodities (raw materials) like gold, silver, crops and livestock, and real estate. They tend to do well when inflation accelerates.

Long-term bonds pay a fixed interest rate for a fixed number of years.

Cash investments pay low interest rates but are readily accessible. Short-term bonds, money market funds, and short-term bank certificates of deposit are included in the cash category.

Stocks and inflation-hedges offer the highest investment returns but are also the riskiest. Cash and long-term bonds are the safest but provide lower returns. However, if you have money in each of the four categories, you'll always be gaining with some of them. Also, remember Professor Sharpe's conclusion—aiming to beat the market rather than accept it typically yields lower gains.

I recommend investing your money in a group of "index funds." Importantly, the money you put in these funds should be separate from money you keep on hand for emergencies. Index funds are collections of individual investments in a specific category. They are designed to reflect the entire investment category. For example, a stock index fund could hold hundreds of individual stocks.

A major benefit of index funds is their low fees—usually under 0.5%. This compares to fees four to six times higher—sometimes more—for professional financial advisers like stockbrokers and financial planners. There are several well-known companies offering index funds, such as Vanguard, Fidelity, and Schwab.

You should distribute your investments among index funds representing the four major investment categories. However, your distribution should vary with your age. Why? Because the level of investment risk you take varies with your age. When you're young and just starting your career and family, you face many uncertainties. Your life simply isn't settled. You need to be cautious in investing and take little risk. But when your career is established, and especially when your kids have left the nest, you can take more risks in investing. Then, when you retire and need to rely on your investments, you return to lower-risk investments.

TABLE 8

Percentage of Total Investments in Each Category
Over the Life-Cycle Recommended by the Author.

Investment Type	Early-Career 20s- early 30s	Mid-Career Late 30s- early 50s	Late Career Mid 50s- Mid 60s	Retirement Late 60s +
Stocks	20%	55%	40%	10%
Inflation Hedges	10%	25%	15%	5%
Long-term Bonds	20%	10%	25%	25%
Cash	50%	10%	20%	60%

TABLE 9

Percentage of Total Investments in Each Category Over
the Life-Cycle Recommended by Professor Malkiel.

Investment Type	Early-Career 20s- early 30s	Mid-Career Late 30s- early 50s	Late Career Mid 50s- Mid 60s	Retirement Late 60s +
Stocks	70%	65%	55%	40%
Inflation Hedges	10%	10%	12.5%	15%
Long-term Bonds	15%	20%	27.5%	35%
Cash	5%	5%	5%	10%

Source: Malkiel, Burton, *A Random Walk Down Wall Street,* 15th Edition, 2023.

Table 8 gives my suggested distribution of investment funds through four stages of your life. The four investment types line up by their level of risk, with stocks being the riskiest and cash being the least. Notice that in both your early career and again in retirement most of the investments are in the low-risk categories of long-term bonds and cash. Conversely, in both mid-career and late career, the higher risk investments—stocks, inflation hedges—have the largest shares.

The percentages in Table 8 indicate not only how you allocate new investment money, but also the targets for the distribution of your total investments in each category. This means that at the end of each year, you may need to adjust your investment amounts between categories to achieve the percentages.

In fairness, I should point out that experts disagree on the distribution of investments during your life. In Table 9, I show you the recommendations of Professor Burton Malkiel, a legend in financial analysis. His famous book, *A Random Walk Down Wall Street*, is currently in its 15th edition. The key difference between Tables 2 and 3 is Professor Malkiel's higher allocation to stocks both in a person's younger years and older years. My allocations are more risk-averse in those years. Still, Professor Malkiel and I both recommend diversifying your investments rather than trying to "beat the market," and using index funds.

You can decide which recommendation best reflects your tradeoff for "return versus risk." My allocation focuses more on reducing risk but also potentially sacrificing what you earn. Professor Malkiel does the opposite.

CHAPTER 3

How to Receive Your Investment Money

For several investment objectives, this is an easy question to answer. You save for five years in order to make a down payment on a home. At the end of the five years, you withdraw the money, make the down payment, and purchase the home.

Or, you save for your child's college tuition over fifteen years. Then, at the beginning of each of the four years your child is in college, you withdraw money and pay the tuition.

In the first chapter I gave an example of another important investment goal—saving for retirement. The example had you saving for 35 years while working, and then using those savings during 30 years in retirement. The problem is, what if you live longer than 30 years in retirement? With this example, you'd have no money left.

Fortunately, there's a special way to receive money set aside for retirement. It's called buying an annuity, and it works like this.

You've saved money for retirement and now you're ready to retire. You take the money you've saved and buy an annuity. The annuity promises to pay you a certain amount per period (such as a month) for as long as you live. After you pass, you can designate that the payments continue to your spouse or another beneficiary as long as they live.

How can a company do this? It's because the companies that operate annuities are insurance firms. They use mortality tables to balance people who outlive the average mortality for their age—thereby resulting in the company losing money on the contract—against people who die before their average mortality—meaning the company gains money on that contract.

Think of annuities as the opposite of life insurance. With life insurance, you make regular payments over time and then your beneficiaries receive a large dollar amount when you die. With an annuity, you pay the insurance company a large dollar amount today and then receive regular payments for as long as you live.

The kind of annuity I've described is an "immediate annuity." You give the insurance company the cash you've saved for retirement, and the monthly income for your retirement begins immediately. The monthly payments will continue for as long as you live, and they can be extended for as long as your spouse lives if your spouse outlives you. Of course, the payments will be smaller in this case.

There are two reasons why more people don't use annuities for their retirement income. The first is they worry about dying too soon and having the insurance company "make money" from them. The second is that they want any money they don't use for their retirement to go to beneficiaries like their children or grandchildren.

These concerns are understandable. There are annuities that will continue to pay a designated beneficiary your monthly annuity income for a limited number of years if you and your spouse have both died. Alternatively, a lump sum amount can be paid to the beneficiary. But including these types of provisions in the annuity will, again, result in lower monthly annuity income while you are living.

That being said, there is one provision I strongly recommend for an annuity: an annual inflation adjustment. Without this provision, the monthly income from your annuity stays the same regardless of inflation, meaning your annuity dollars would buy less and less each year as prices increase. Inflation always occurs—it's just a matter of how much. Even a modest annual inflation rate of 2% results in a 22% decline of the dollar's purchasing power over a decade. Some annuities allow an annual inflation adjustment to an index like the Consumer Price Index (CPI); others make you pick an annual inflation rate. I prefer the CPI Index, but if it is not available, choose 3% for the annual rate to hedge your bets.

There are two other features of immediate annuities I recommend looking into. You'll need to consider fees, or the percentage of your investment the insurance company will take. You will, of course, want the lowest fees. Secondly, note the risk rating of the insurance company offering you the annuity. Insurance companies can take too much risk, be mismanaged, or just be unlucky. There are three rating agencies that measure the risk of the companies: AM Best, S&P, and Moody's. Only choose annuities from insurance companies with the highest ratings—A+ for AM Best and S&P, and Aaa for Moody's.

To investigate what your monthly income will be from an immediate annuity, visit http://www.*immediateannuities.com*. This website allows you to input the lump sum investment amount you are putting into the annuity as well as features such as beneficiaries and inflation adjustments. It then estimates your first-year monthly income paid from the annuity offered by several alternative companies alongside their ratings from the three ratings services.

But what amount should you use for your lump sum investment amount? All you need to do is look back at the retirement program you ran and go to the entry "After-Tax Amount at Retiring." The entry tells you how much you will have accumulated after paying the taxes due at withdrawal (only for the Regular IRA, 401K, 403B, and Keogh plans) to purchase an immediate annuity. Also, in using the computer program at *immediateannuities.com*, select the "savings" option, since the calculations in the three *Retirement Saving*" computer programs already adjust for any taxes paid when converting your lump sum investment amount to an immediate annuity.

You may find the calculated monthly annuity amount will be less than what you estimated was needed. This is because the annuity gives you unlimited payments, whereas the calculations in the *Retirement Saving* programs are based on a specific number of years in retirement. If this situation occurs and you want the annuity amount to equal what you need, simply increase the dollar amount used in the *Retirement Saving* program by the proportional difference between what you need and what the annuity will provide. For example, if you need $38,400 ($3,200 per month) but the annuity will only pay $36,000 ($3,000 per month), increase your amount to save by 6.7% ($38,400/$36,000).

Final Words

I hope this short book has given you some guidance on saving, investing, and receiving your hard-earned money. As you have seen, the essentials can be easily grasped. You also now have access to computer programs for calculations based on your personal situation that will help you as you continue to plan your future.

Does this mean you never have to consult with a professional, like a stockbroker, financial planner, or insurance agent? For some of you, the answer is "yes"—you can run your financial life on your own. Others may still want to work with a professional, and in my opinion, that is entirely reasonable. I know many talented, honest, and plain-speaking persons in this field. And now you have the knowledge and understanding to follow and evaluate the financial recommendations they offer you. After all, as has been said many, many times: knowledge is power.

APPENDIX

Detailed Provisions of Retirment Saving Plans

(Dollar amounts are for 2023)

Feature	Typical Investment	Regular IRA, 401K, 403B, Keogh	Roth IRA
Who Can Participate	Anyone	Anyone for a Regular IRA Workers in private firms that offer 401K plans Workers of educational, religious and non-profit institutions that offer 403B plans Self-employed persons for Keogh plans	Anyone
Income Limits on Contributors	None	None	Can be used for single taxpayer with income up to $153,000, or married jointly filing taxpayer with income up to $214,000.
Limits on Annual Contribution Amounts	None	For a Regular IRA: $6,500 if under 50; $7,500 if 50 or over For 401K and 403B: $22,000 if under 50; $30,000 if 50 or over Keogh: 25% of earnings or $66,000, whichever is less	$6,500 if under age 50; $7,500 if 50 or over If have both Regular IRA and Roth IRA, combined contributions are limited to $6,500 if under age 50 and $7,500 if 50 or over

Feature	Typical Investment	Regular IRA, 401K, 403B, Keogh	Roth IRA
Taxation of Annual Contribution	Taxed	None	Taxed
Taxation of Earnings	Taxed	None	None
Taxation of Withdrawals	None	Yes	None
Withdrawal Requirements	None	10% penalty if withdraw before age 59.5; Must begin withdrawing by age 72, or age 73 if are 73 after Dec. 31, 2022; must use minimum required amounts or face penalty of 50% on amount under-withdrawn	10% penalty if withdraw before age 59.5; otherwise, none until death of owner

Note all dollar amounts are for 2023. Typically, these amounts are increased each year by the rate of inflation. For example, if the inflation rate in 2023 is 4%, then the dollar amounts will increase by 4% in 2024.

Also, while you can use several tax-favored savings plans together, there are still annual contribution limits. For example, you can have both a Regular IRA and a Roth IRA, but the combined contribution to both must follow the same limits of $6,500 if you are under 50 and $7,500 if you are 50 and over. You can also have either IRA and a 401K or a 403B as long as you stick to the annual contribution limits for each.

About the Author

Michael Walden, Ph.D., is a William Neal Reynolds Distinguished Professor Emeritus at North Carolina State University and President of Walden Economic Consulting, LLC. During his 43-year career on the faculty at NC State, Walden became recognized as an expert on the macro-economy, public policy, and personal finance. He is the author of fourteen books and over 330 articles and reports, and he has made 3,200 personal appearances. Walden is also a frequent contributor to the national and local media and has appeared on all the major national news outlets. He continues to write a biweekly newspaper column distributed throughout North Carolina. Walden has served on several public committees and commissions, including the "Future of Wake County" and the NC FIRST Transportation Commission. Walden was an adviser to North Carolina's Governor during the pandemic. He has won numerous awards, including two Champion-Tuck Awards for Excellence in

Broadcasting, the UNC Board of Governors Award for Excellence in Public Service, the Holladay Medal for Excellence from North Carolina State University, and the Order of the Long Leaf Pine. Walden is a member of the North Carolina Economic Development Association, and he resides in Raleigh with his wife, Mary.